Corals

by Lola M. Schaefer

Consulting Editor: Gail Saunders-Smith, Ph.D.

Consultant: Jody Byrum, Science Writer,
SeaWorld Education Department

Pebble Books

an imprint of Capstone Press
Mankato, Minnesota

Pebble Books are published by Capstone Press
818 North Willow Street, Mankato, Minnesota 56001
http://www.capstone-press.com

Library of Congress Cataloging-in-Publication Data
Schaefer, Lola M., 1950–
　　Corals/by Lola M. Schaefer.
　　p. cm.—(Ocean life)
　　Includes bibliographical references (p. 23) and index.
　　Summary: Simple text and photographs depict corals and how they create
coral reefs.
　　ISBN 0-7368-0244-4
　　1. Corals—Juvenile literature. [1. Corals. 2. Coral reefs and islands.] I. Title.
II. Series: Schaefer, Lola M., 1950–　Ocean life.
QL377.C5S354　　　1999
593.6—dc21　　　　　　　　　　　　　　　　　　　　　　98-40905
　　　　　　　　　　　　　　　　　　　　　　　　　　　　　　CIP
　　　　　　　　　　　　　　　　　　　　　　　　　　　　　　AC

Note to Parents and Teachers

The Ocean Life series supports national science standards for units
on the diversity and unity of life. The series shows that animals
have features that help them live in different environments. This
book describes corals and illustrates how they create coral reefs. The
photographs support early readers in understanding the text. The
repetition of words and phrases helps early readers learn new
words. This book also introduces early readers to subject-specific
vocabulary words, which are defined in the Words to Know section.
Early readers may need assistance to read some words and to use
the Table of Contents, Words to Know, Read More, Internet Sites,
and Index/Word List sections of the book.

2

Table of Contents

Corals are ocean animals.

6

Corals live together
in colonies.

Corals can be many colors.

10

Corals have tentacles.

12

Corals catch food with their tentacles.

Soft corals and hard corals are two kinds of corals.

16

Soft corals have soft bodies.

skeleton

Hard corals have hard outer skeletons.

Some hard corals grow into coral reefs.

Words to Know

colony—a large group of animals that live together

coral—an ocean animal with a soft body and many tentacles; corals often live in groups.

coral reef—an area of coral skeletons and rocks near the surface of the ocean; corals join their bodies together and attach to coral reefs.

ocean—a large body of salt water; coral reefs grow well in areas of the ocean that have warm, shallow water.

skeleton—a structure that supports and protects the soft body of an animal; some corals have hard outer skeletons.

tentacle—a long arm of an animal; corals use tentacles to catch food.

Read More

Cerullo, Mary M. *Coral Reef: A City That Never Sleeps.* New York: Cobblehill Books, 1996.

Fowler, Allan. *It Could Still Be Coral.* Rookie Read-About Science. New York: Children's Press, 1996.

Scarborough, Kate. *Coral Reef.* Watch It Grow. Alexandria, Va.: Time-Life Books, 1997.

Internet Sites

Coral Reef
http://www.germantown.k12.il.us/html/coral.html

Fisheye View Cam
http://www.FisheyeView.com/Recent.html

Marine Invertebrates of Hawaii
http://www2.hawaii.edu/~tissot/inverts/inverts.htm

Sea and Sky: Reef Life
http://www.seasky.org/sea2.html

Index/Word List

Word Count: 51
Early-Intervention Level: 10

Editorial Credits

Martha E. Hillman, editor; Steve Christensen, cover designer and illustrator; Kimberly Danger and Sheri Gosewisch, photo researchers

Photo Credits

Craig D. Wood, 6

Jay Ireland and Georgienne Bradley, cover, 1, 10, 14

Photo Network/Hal Beral, 8; Howard Hall, 20

Tom Stack & Associates/Dave B. Fleetham, 4, 16; Brian Parker, 12, 18